BEHOLDING

HIS

FACE

BEHOLDING HIS FACE

**ESSAYS AND POEMS ON THE WAR
BETWEEN OUR OLD AND NEW NATURES**

ALMA NEWITT

Prepared for publication by Kelly Mangione

Memoir by Laura Johnson

Foreword by Ann Sullivan

Scripture quotations marked NIV are taken from the Holy Bible, New International Version®, NIV® Copyright © 1973, 1978, 1984, 2011 by Biblica, Inc.

Scripture quotations marked KJV are taken from the KING JAMES VERSION (KJV) by Public Domain.

Scripture quotations marked NKJV are taken from The Holy Bible, New King James Version Copyright © 1982 by Thomas Nelson, Inc.

Scripture quotations marked Amplified Bible are taken from the Amplified Bible (AMP), Copyright © 1954, 1958, 1962, 1964, 1965, 1987 by The Lockman Foundation.

ISBN-13: 978-0615961699 (Custom Universal)
ISBN-10: 061596169X

For Worldwide Distribution, Printed in U.S.A.

MEMOIR

When I was born again in 1967, God gave me a mother and her name is Alma. I've always found this interesting because my natural mother's name was Alva. My own mother had a mental illness which caused her not to be able to be emotionally close to me. God was so good to me, providing Alma, because she was always kind and loving and perfect for me. She "loved me to life" over the years. I could not have picked a better person for me.

She was quiet in nature and gentle. She had a very calming influence. She loved words and was so open to God and his creativity, and she was always listening. She could create the coziest atmospheres, like you were walking into a fairy land. Her homes were so magical, like the "three Bears" house. She made people feel welcome.

Although Alma did not have natural children, she had many children: sons, daughters, grandsons, granddaughters, sisters and brothers. She loved people and didn't see race color or age. She fought for the underdog and spent many hours in prayer. At times she would even put a chair in her closet where she would sit and pray to set herself away from the noises of the world to be closer to Him. She encouraged me to do the same.

Over the years her cry has been, "your will be done." Indeed, God has used her mightily in so many ways, and so many lives, touching them with his love. She would often say, "Pray, Laura. Let's pray, dear." She always pointed up. She loved to gather with the saints of God and wait on him. If you weren't use to the silence she loved, it could be awkward, because you would be all alone with your own thoughts. But if you were still long enough, you could enter another realm of sensitivity and prayer.

In love and honesty, she gave ceaselessly of herself as a friend, helper, encourager, counselor, and vessel of God's grace to all who crossed her path. I have been privileged to have my life knitted together with Alma's for all these years and I am richer and stronger for having been blessed by her precious life. She loved me in all my broken places.

Alma is still alive, just living at a new address, and we will join her again one day when God calls each of us home.

-Laura Johnson

CONTENTS

FOREWORD

Alma was a devoted housewife who turned away from the allure of fame and fortune and surrendered her life to Christ and the pursuit of holiness. She became a powerful prayer warrior who yearned to seek him early. She was always ready to go to battle, often calling the saints together to wait on God and pray. Alma was the "Mother Theresa" of our community, reaching out to all and calling them into her heart and home to hear the good news, that no matter the circumstance, Jesus was the answer. Alma's relationship with the Lord allowed her the inspiration to find and bring me to Christ at a dangerously pivotal time in my life. Because of her, my life and family and for generations to come, will never be the same! Alma's devotion to God helped countless other people as well and for that reason, she has been a tremendous light and inspiration to many, and will continue to be to all who learn of her life example.

Through the ups and downs of my messy life Alma was my spiritual "mother" and a friend that stuck closer than a brother always speaking words of truth and life and reminding me to "go into my closet and cry out to Jesus". She would call often and ask if I had a few minutes for her to read me one of her poems or essays. For many years I was blessed with these writings and encouraged Alma to publish a book so that others could benefit too. Alma, being the creative type, was overwhelmed at the thought of putting her writings in order. For two summers we spent precious time together beginning the process. I had only made a dent in this project when the Lord moved me away from my dear Alma and I was no longer able to help her. I remember, as I argued with God at the idea of moving, that I was needed to publish her book. As always, He had a better, more perfect plan. My daughter Kelly took over where I left off and became a true catalyst in bringing this book into reality. She was transformed as she spent six months and many hours working closely with Alma, being deeply touched by the presence of God in and through her life.

Alma's writings have a way of reaching the deepest part of our hearts, revealing truth, and bringing light and life. Each essay came from her daily personal struggle and deep desire to be more of who God called her to be, never satisfied to be mediocre. Filled with insight into the constant struggle between the flesh and the spirit, they hold a timeless message of hope and encouragement to turn our eyes away from self to the only One who can satisfy. As you read you will connect with this deep cry to overcome and surrender to His way in your everyday life and circumstances. You will be strengthened and encouraged for the journey as you allow the Lord to impact your heart with the truth He spoke through my dearest friend, Alma.

-Ann Sullivan

PREFACE

Many years ago I had an experience which should have alerted me to a trap I was falling into. I was a fairly new Christian and had been touched by great grace but I had wandered into the wilderness of self-help. An early saint once wrote that all Christians can be divided by type into two categories. One group looks at God so intently that they never notice their own faults. The other is so intent on their weaknesses that they lose sight of God. I am definitely of the latter group. After the initial glory of the presence of Christ faded from my experience I became vividly aware of the things that were still wrong with me—laziness, self-indulgence, sensitive pride, etc. And I thought I had to re-form my self to be pleasing to God. I read lots of books about Him, tried to get up at 5 am to pray but failed most of the time, even attended a sort of self-help group that urged you to observe and "work" on your self. All of these things helped make me believe I was still my old self and paved the way for the theft of the new identity I had been given in Christ.

One evening during this period our church hosted a speaker who was reputed to have gifts of the Spirit. As I was getting ready to go to the meeting I picked up a large hand mirror my mother had given me and looked at my face and then for a time searched for any spots and wrinkles. When I got to the meeting people were still milling about and a woman who was apparently the speaker came up to me and said, as I arrived, the Lord had shown her a picture of me looking at my face in a mirror and He wanted me to know He wished me to look at his face and He would show me what was wrong with me and if I didn't see it He would send hornets.

Needless to say, I was shocked to hear this woman's accurate words and marveled at them for some time. I wondered what the hornets might be but I really didn't take the advice to heart and the clarity of the memory eventually faded. It was only recently that it came to mind again when three companies treated us unfairly and attacked like hornets one right after the other with such repetitive force that I couldn't help but notice vindictiveness in my nature I had never seen in all my own self-examination.

Scripture tells us that the gifts of the Spirit are given to build us up in Christ. The word of knowledge given to me so long ago told me to behold the Lord's face and not my own. Many of the essays and poems that follow deal with the struggle between these two faces. They span many years and topics. I didn't set out to write them— they seemed to come as circumstances of life came. It is my hope and prayer that they may encourage both reader and writer to spend more time in his Presence so that *"we all with open face beholding as in a glass the glory of the Lord are changed into the same image from glory to glory even as by the Spirit of the Lord."*[1]

-Alma Newitt

---

[1] *2 Corinthians 3:18 (KJV)*

Forging ahead,
hammering
empires of iron,
blacksmiths, we.
When we might have been
wading in rivers
of living water,
sifting for gold.

GLIMPSE OF GLORY

Some years ago I met a person who had such a glow on her face that I felt compelled to ask about it. She was in the midst of moving and a mutual friend had asked me to return something to her before she left town. Though she was very busy, she responded to my question and took time to tell me her story.

She had been an abused child with an alcoholic father and ran away from home at an early age. A number of therapists had treated her for severe depression. There had been a succession of unhappy affairs. Finally, when a lover who was also her spiritual guru abandoned her, she broke down and her psychiatrist wasn't able to reach the depths of her despair.

One day when she was near suicide, her landlady told her if she gave her life to Jesus, He would help her. The young woman had previously disdained this "simplistic solution", but in her desperation she turned to Him and experienced an overwhelming sense of his reality. After this she began to read the Bible and attend church. Then she stopped seeing her psychiatrist. Her concerned landlady felt that this was a mistake, that she still needed counseling. The young woman reassured her she wasn't giving up counseling, just switching counselors. She had read Jesus' words, *"come to me, all you who are weary and burdened, and I will give you rest,"*[2] and she was going to go to Him instead of her psychiatrist.

After that, when times of depression came, she would

---

[2] *Matthew 11:28 (NIV)*

6

stretch out on the floor face down and pour out all the grief and anguish of her heart. Then she would wait in his presence until her burden was lifted. I asked her how long she waited. She said many hours sometimes.

As I looked at the peace and radiance of this woman's countenance, I realized she had discovered the secret of transformation. God's strength was being perfected in her weakness. Again and again she brought the lead of her pain and waited for the divine alchemist to change it to gold. And in the process, the nature of Christ had begun to manifest through her. I never saw this young woman again and our mutual friend lost track of her, so I know nothing more of her journey. But she remains vivid in my memory because the glory I saw in her made me homesick for the kingdom of heaven.

If you will bring
your leaden state
He will give you gold.
But you must wait.
It takes time
to melt your mettle down.
It takes time
to make a golden crown.

COME APART OR COME APART

Recollection is a wonderful word. It speaks of a state of integration when the bits and pieces of our fragmented beings are "re-collected" and there is a sense of greater wholeness or oneness with God.

All of ordinary life seems calculated to scatter us—the dirty house that always needs cleaning, the ringing telephone, the broken down car, the crying child, the TV news alert, and on and on, sometimes all at once demanding our attention.

If we are living in the shallow, heady self, harried by people and events and our reactions to them, it's all too much and we come apart at the seams. It is then we must take our shattered state and return home for repair. We are not like Humpty Dumpty who couldn't be put together. We have a King who will take our broken pieces and make us whole again.

Coming apart from time to time is essential for our daily spiritual health. John Wesley's mother had so many children she couldn't get away, but at certain periods of the day she would put her apron over her head and her children wouldn't bother her because they knew she was communing with God. Jesus himself rose early in the morning and spent whole nights in prayer. If the Lord of our faith found this necessary, how much more do we need to come apart so we don't come apart from Him?

Remember Me
in activity
when harried voices cry
and sometimes sigh,
"I must get it done – achieve!"
Stop then, listen, believe,
and rest in Me.
I will work and you just be.

NEED

The need of man opens the heart of God. This is the place where the flow of life begins. While man thinks he is sufficient, there is no flow. He is clogged, full of himself. But when he is empty, poor, naked, and knows he is blind, then Life comes and rivers of living water flow over and through him.

Need is a rich, divine gift. Why do we run from it ashamed and hide it in darkness? If we will bring it to Light, God will provide a hundred-fold provision for our need.

Grace is the ocean
that fills our small
bottles of need.

Filled with the air
of our egos,
we bob and bounce
on the waves,
struggling to keep afloat.

But when enough air
has gone out of us,
the water of Life enters
and fills out bottles of need
until we sink and merge
into the ocean of Grace.

OPEN DOOR

Yesterday I heard a plaintive cry from our little cat. She had been out all night and sounded hungry and eager to get into the house. Though I am presently in a wheelchair with a broken ankle, I tried with considerable difficulty to reach the door outside and let her in. As I was struggling to get to her the thought came to me—if I responded like this to the cry of a cat, how much more does the heavenly father respond to the cries of his children? I finally reached the outside door and when I opened it there was our dear little cat—with a dead bird in its mouth. Quickly I shut the door before she could get in and another thought came—Is this also the way it is with God? He answers our cries, opens the door to his presence and then has to shut it because we have dead birds in our mouths.

I wonder what my dead birds are—Judgments that kill another's spirit? Self-pity that poisons my own soul? Hatred toward someone who has offended me?

I cannot control
this one called "me"
but within my soul
is power to free
from bondage and gloom
and sore despair,
from demonic doom
and powers of air.

My creature is wild
and must be tamed
by Presence of Child
whose being is famed.
Known as Christ Jesus
he dwells in me
in hidden recess
where no one can see

Lord, when my members
would lead me to shame,
may I remember
to call on Your Name.

FAITHFULNESS

I used to think wistfully of the word "faithful" because I knew it wasn't in my nature to be that way. I admired people who were, the dutiful, rain-or-shine "there" ones. I marveled at their solid regularity and lamented my own flighty inconsistency.

When I came to Christ I hoped I would change, but I didn't. For a time I was fairly consistent in following; at other times I would forget about any discipline. But then one day in the midst of much self-pity a new light of understanding was graciously given me. I saw that the word "faithful" actually means full of faith. And for me that meant to be full of faith in God. I had always looked to my self to be something—a faithful dutiful person, when really the word was centered in Him. It was true that my flesh nature was whimsical and undependable. If I looked at the word "faithful" as a human quality, I could never be that way. But if the word means being full of faith in the One who is dependable, there is hope for ones like me.

And is it even possible that the weak nature I have grieved about—could it somehow be a gift to draw me away from leaning on my self, to leaning on the One who never changes?

Lord, here I am.
Foolish, unfaithful,
dumb and blind.

What can You do
with a child like this?
Are there schools for
spiritually retarded
delinquents like me?

Where do you send us?

Ah, yes,

          Earth.

BEARING WITH THE
BURDEN OF ANOTHER

Recently I heard someone describe another as the type of person one "sets oneself up on". This use of words was fresh to me and I saw more clearly a process that often happens unconsciously. We "set ourselves up" by looking down on the weaknesses of others.

I have a friend who reacts violently whenever adult women look to her for support. She is essentially sympathetic to them, but when they begin to lean on her she cuts off in a manner I often feel is merciless. My friend's behavior lulls me into feeling superior. Actually, it's not her behavior, of course, but my reaction to it. I "set myself up" on the pedestal of her weakness. "Why can't she be kinder? Why must she act so harshly to those looking to her for help?" To overcome her fault seems easy to my judgmental self, because it never occurs to that part of me that my friend is bound; that in childhood her mother leaned on her for help to such an extent that her circuits are still overloaded. I think it should be easy for her to correct her behavior, not understanding the chains that keep her in prison.

This same friend has a marvelous facility with money. She knows how to save and manage her finances and yet gives generously. She is critical of another friend who is somewhat of a tightwad. She doesn't understand that the trauma he felt during the depression when his parents had no money has scarred him for life. This friend in turn has a great strength in dealing equitably with others. He is patient and kind no matter how they act. He shakes his head at the impatience and temper tantrums of still another friend. He can't understand her irascible behavior because he doesn't have her temperament.

And this same fiery friend can't understand why I am so "watery-willed" and why I often don't do the things I plan to do. It's easy for her to set her mind on a goal and then work methodically toward its accomplishment. She doesn't realize that "stick-to-itiveness" was lacking even in my childhood and following through on things is not as easy for me as it is for her.

By nature there are some things harder for each of us. Will we go on feeling superior because we don't have the same faults as others? Will we go on "setting ourselves up" on their weaknesses? Or will we *bear one another's burdens, and so fulfill the law of Christ*[3]?

---

[3] *Galatians 6:2-4 (NKJV)*

Mercy and Judgment
like twin sisters
reside in the Womb together.
Joined by their Maker,
they are inseparable;
their union indissoluble,
twined by the same cord of Love.

DEAD RIGHT

I have a friend who gets hysterical if you disagree with her opinion. Another gets hostile at the slightest hint of criticism. Still another, when he makes a mistake, acts as if it never happened. My own shortcomings tend to embarrass me, and I freely admit them to avoid the judgment of others.

But essentially my friends and I are alike. We all want to be right and desperately fear being wrong. Different symptoms, same disease... idolatry. We are worshipping at the altar of our self-image. We say we look to Christ for our righteousness but unconsciously our eyes are on the perfect self we want to be, or the fool we fear we are. Jesus advised us to live in Him. Instead, we are living in the shifting sands of self. This makes us feel shaky. Somewhere inside we sense something is wrong. That is why we have to continually prove to ourselves and others that we are "right".

We have forgotten that only One is right and our only hope of being right is living in Him and receiving his rightness.

God, deliver me
from my own righteousness
which stinks like skunk cabbage
rising from the earth.
Give me Your righteousness
that falls from Above
like cleansing rain.

IMAGES

Self-images seem like the contemporary counterpart for the idols of the Old Testament. Positive self-images help us to function better in life. I am confident in my own ability to cope. I have faith in myself. A negative self-image makes living less easy. I have a sense of being inadequate and not able to cope with things very well. I do not have faith in my self.

Even though the positive self-image makes passage through this present world less painful, it is no different essentially from the negative self-image in relation to the next world. If the purpose of life is relationship with God, then having a positive or negative self-image is beside the point. It is faith in Christ that matters. I am not looking to my self for power to live life. Rather, looking to Christ in me for strength to get through this world is what deepens my bonds with Him.

So if I look to my self-fearing and mourning my inadequacy or look to my self with faith—it is the same. *"Without faith in God it is impossible to please Him..."*[4] It is believing, or as the original Greek puts it, leaning on Him that counts.

---

[4] *Hebrews 11:6 (KJV)*

As long as we are
strong somebodies
there is no room
for Him in our inn.
Christ comes to
weak nobodies
who cry for help
in their low estate.

WHAT AM I PROVING?

I am daily presented with the choice of living for self or living for God in me. Will I try to prove myself today? My adequacy? My superiority? Will I even use God to help me prove myself—enlisting his aid so that I may not appear the fool that I am?

Or will I live by God – and prove Him and his adequacy? He has said He is able and willing to answer every need of his children. Will I lean on Him and his promises? Or will I look to my self and figure and scheme and worry?

The book of Malachi says:

> *"Bring all the tithes…into the storehouse, that there may be food in My house, and prove Me now by it, says the Lord of hosts, if I will not open the windows of heaven for you and pour you out a blessing, that there shall not be room enough to receive it."*[5]

Yet why do some of us who have, so to speak, "brought our tithes" and given our lives to Christ continue to try to prove ourselves? It is as if we are poor urchins who encounter a wondrous King who adopts us into his royal line. And then we forget our new identity as children of the King and think we are still poor urchins who must fend for ourselves and become somebodies.

---

[5] *Malachi 3:10 (Amplified Bible)*

Am I a self-centered somebody? Or is it God who is the Somebody I am centered in? Is the secret drive of my life to prove my self and my own prowess in some arena or other? Or has this been replaced with the desire to prove Him and His magnificent adequacy and power?

Which is it?

Hungry for accomplishment,
ravenous for praise:
squandering substance,
wasting days.

Or

Hungry for the Word of Life,
giving God the praise:
feeding on his substance,
walking in his ways.

ON RECEIVING CRITICISM

Most of us don't do well with criticism. We certainly
don't welcome it. But maybe we should, because our
response to it is an indicator of where we're living inside.
Jesus told us that we should live in Him. Often we
imagine we are living in Him when we're actually in the
old flesh nature. Criticism brings us to the reality of our
position. It is easy to confess with our mouths that
Christ is our righteousness and we have none of our own.
We can even in the abstract admit we're not perfect.
But, dare somebody suggest we talk too much or aren't
as good as they are, and we want to clobber them.

Underneath, most of us are all too aware of our faults
and long to be different. We even pray to be changed; to
decrease that Christ might increase. But when the
instrument for the operation begins, we don't make the
connection between our prayer and their cutting
criticism. A person's critical words and attitude of
superiority hurt. It makes us mad to be treated like an
idiot, a nobody. We can receive this blow and die a little
or draw the sword and defend our good image. If we
choose to hit back or lick our wounds with self-pity, or
have our friends salve them with sympathy; or scurry
around pleasing people so they won't criticize us, or
write off the critic, the whole point of the matter has
been missed. We have prayed to decrease that Christ
might increase in us, and when someone cuts us down a
size, we forget we
asked for it.

It is vital that we connect our prayers with the slams and hurts that come in our relationship with others, so that our wounds will bring us to Him. "Here is my pain, Lord. What are you saying to me?" And as we ask, we will see that behind the proud sister and the scornful brother, there is his transforming Love seeking to answer our request for change. Understanding this, we will then be able to receive criticism as a gift from God.

How much pain
must one go through
before the will
conforms to You;
before the moments
and the days
flow through the life
with ceaseless praise?

WHAT AM I LOOKING AT?

King David *"saw the Lord always before"*[6] him.
What do I always see before me?

Is it an image of my self the way I want to be?
Is it an image of my self the way I fear I am?
Is it an image of my self the way my parents wanted me to be?
Is it an image of my self the way I think others see me?

Are these images like ghosts that rattle around in our unconscious, making us continually uneasy? In any case they obscure our vision of God.

If we are pre-occupied with these images, there is no room for Christ in our consciousness. Jesus said, *"I am with you always."*[7] As we take time to be with Him and dwell on his words of living truth, it will help loosen the bondage of self-images and enable us to *"look unto Jesus the author and finisher of our faith."*[8]

---

[6] *Acts 2:25 (NIV)*
[7] *Matthew 28:20 (KJV)*
[8] *Hebrews 12:2 (KJV)*

O God,
help me to build my life
on the rock of your Presence
not on the shifting sands
of my self.

MY SELF IS NOT WHO I AM

From my earliest days I remember wanting to be the best and have the best of everything. Other people were not real to me, merely breathing objects to facilitate the desires of my self. As I grew older, this attitude continued but under more polite acceptable wrappings. It was only when I encountered the reality of the living Christ that things changed for me. A whole new world opened up. I experienced the glorious Love and forgiveness of the One whose arms are open to all men. Suddenly I could see other people were real. I could see their need and feel compassion for them. But the same Love that revealed the reality of others also revealed the reality of my self. I saw that I was not a nice person; I was selfish to the core.

At first the glory that I was a new creature was so intense that the sight of my self in all its unglory didn't bother me. I was forgiven! But as the feeling of the Lords presence and his forgiveness receded, I was left with my self—and my self was not pretty, much less happy. I felt guilty thinking it must be my fault that the glory disappeared. What had I done or not done? I read Jesus' words *"Be perfect, therefore, as your heavenly Father is perfect."*[9] For years I tried hard to be perfect but of course never succeeded, and my left arm actually got cold because I was trying to cut off the "bad" part of me.

---

[9] *Matthew 5:48 (NIV)*

How like the enemy of our souls to try to spoil the magnificent work begun in the Spirit by making us think we have been abandoned by God because we are not good enough. And then getting us to labor on the endless treadmill of self improvement that leads no where. What a dilemma! We feel God does not accept us because we are imperfect and all our strivings don't effect the perfect spiritual facelift we think we need.

We have forgotten the good news that was once so real to us. We are forgiven—whether we <u>feel</u> it or not—the blood of Christ has redeemed us with all our sins and weaknesses. We are "accepted in the Beloved" because of God's unfathomable Love manifested in the Cross.

Our self is no longer who we are—we are new creatures in Christ!

Your way, not my way
is the cry of my deepest heart.
But sadly, that is not all of me,
there is another part.
Self shouts, "I want to be free!"
Not your way, my way it must be!"
Help, Lord.
Weaken that other part,
strengthen my deepest heart.

DIVINE EXCHANGE

In the outer parts of our nature there are strong holds
that keep Christ from coming through. What are the
opposing forces, the weapons of war that keep my Lord a
prisoner within? What bastions of pride? What
battalions of lust?

Christ is a prisoner of war within me.
What can I give to get Him out?
What can I pay that He may be free?

There is only one coin;
heavier than lead,
stronger than iron.
It is called self.
Self must be exchanged,
and taken hostage,
that Christ might live
through me.

IN OR OUT

The other day a friend was describing to me the different
ways her three small sons attempt to get their own way.
One whines and complains, another screams and
demands, and the third tries to woo his mother so she
will do what he wants. My friend has the most difficulty
with the oldest child. She says he is always out for
number one. His form of self will is most like her own
and she hates to see herself in him. In truth, all of them
are "out" for number one.

It is said a child is spoiled if the will is not disciplined by
a certain age. There is certainly truth to this since
unrestrained self-will is harder to deal with later on. But
aren't we all essentially "spoiled" in our carnal natures?
As we leave the age of so-called innocence, most of us
learn to cover over offensive egoism with nice manners,
but underneath the respectable clothing is our common
condition of naked self-will.

Too often those of us who wish to follow Christ fail to
recognize the operation of our self-wills because we dress
them in robes of righteousness. Under the guise of
"speaking the truth" and "doing good", we complain,
coerce and even slander our brethren because they don't
do things the way we want them to.

No matter if we call ourselves Christians, if we live in the
self we are spoiled and want our own way. The Kingdom
of Heaven is within, in that secret place where Christ
dwells. Unless we live there in Him, we will be "out" for
us.

Oh, that will of iron
plated with gold.
How beautiful it looks -
sweet even holy
good and kindly too.
Only when crossed
does it pierce you through.

SELF-CENTERED RELIGION

After God has reached down to us in our desperate state and pulled us up from the quicksand of our ego-worlds, some of us get pulled down again, only this time it is white quicksand we fall into. Our dreams of glory are no longer worldly but spiritual.

A friend and I fell into this trap. We used to ask each other regularly, "Do you think I've grown?" We had both experienced the free grace of Christ, but our eyes turned back to ourselves. We became religious - and forgot God.

The ego or self-nature is very sly. It will do anything to maintain its life—even strive to be holy. It can wear crosses, pray, read the Bible, attend church, preach and teach, and do all manner of good works. Yet its roots are in the earth and its holiness is a brittle thing. In crisis it falls apart and often acts like hell.

The word "holy" in both the Hebrew and Greek means "separate" or "set apart". When we live in the self that Jesus told us to deny, and it "gets religion", we set ourselves apart in a wrong way. We become judgmental of others and preoccupied with our own spiritual life and gifts. We try hard to be holy and our egos continue to grow, their girth hidden in flowing white cloaks of self-righteousness.

When we are separated unto God we live in Christ and our religion is centered in Him. The holiness which comes from being in his presence is full of mercy and compassion. We behold Him as he is and see our selves as we are. After this, how can we help but be merciful to others? Our growth then comes not from self-striving, but from our repentance and His grace. Then we are freed from the bondage of self-centered religion and we understand that relationship with God and reflecting his Love to others is what true religion is all about.

I gave my life
to you once
but then, bit by bit
in barely discernible
increments,
my self took it back.
Hidden under a cloak
of religiosity
it gained sovereignty
by "doing good."

COMING TO HIM

When I'm not just thinking about God, but coming to
Him, everything changes. Just thinking about Him is
thin—it can keep me up in the head. But coming to Him
brings me into relationship here, now. I am dropped
down from the head to the center. When I am there in
the center, feeding on him who is the bread of Life,
everything changes. I begin to breathe deeper, the
waters of my being are calmed, and a peace comes.
*"Seek you first the kingdom of God...and all these things
shall be added to you."*[10] It's amazing how when the
peace comes all the troubling "things" from human
relationships to plumbers and lost keys, all these fall into
a different place; smaller, less anguished, they seem to
take care of themselves. When I my self try to fix
"things" that are awry and seek my own solutions, I am
often left fearful and strained; a turbulent person with
tight muscles and shallow breath.

Medical research increasingly shows the damaging
effects of physical tension and lack of oxygen in our
bodies. So when we seek
the kingdom of God first, it is not just a pious action but
an infinitely practical way of truly healthy living.

---

[10] *Matthew 6:33(KJV)*

I want to live in you, Lord
but I need to know
where you live in me
so I can find my way
to where you are.

Please give me directions
or I will stay lost
in the wilderness
of my self.

WHAT ARE WE EATING?

Some time ago a man who had been through a time of mental and spiritual derangement told me that at a point of extremity he found himself gnawing on his own arm. This terrible and vivid picture stayed with me, but during the past days as I have been reading the sixth chapter of the gospel of John it especially came to mind. In this chapter much is said about food and eating. There is the miraculous feeding of the five thousand and later the admonition of Jesus to his followers that they should work for the bread which will not perish. And then his introduction of Himself, as the Bread sent from heaven which they are to eat.

When he says to his disciples that they must drink his blood and eat his flesh to have true eternal life, we are told that *"many of His disciples drew back and no longer accompanied Him"*[11]. Were the disciples repelled because they took him literally and thought they had to drink real blood and eat real flesh? But he said *"the flesh conveys no benefit, the words that I have been speaking to you are Spirit and Life."*[12] So they must have been reassured then that he wasn't speaking of cannibalistic practice.

The clue perhaps to the disciples leaving Jesus is in verse 64 when he says *"but some of you failed to believe and trust and have faith"*[13] He had just called Himself the

---

[11] *John 6:66 (Amplified Bible)*
[12] *John 6:63 (Amplified Bible)*

41

Bread from heaven—He is no longer just a teacher, a prophet, a miracle worker. Now they must have a total devotion to Him as the anointed one of God, even an absorption of his Life into them signified by eating his flesh and drinking his blood.

When I looked up the Greek words for eating to better understand the references to it, I found the words Jesus used in this gospel—"Phago," which means simply eating and drinking, and "Trogo" which means to gnaw or chew thoroughly. It was then I thought of my friend who at the height of his madness had gnawed on his own arm. Could there be a spiritual parallel to his physical action? And is that what many of us do to some extent much of the time—feed on our own flesh? Was my friend's action just the ultimate physical display of self-absorption? Don't we usually feed on our own thoughts and emotions, dreams and desires, chewing and gnawing our own flesh about what someone did to us, what we want, what we don't have? And Jesus is calling his disciples to be totally absorbed in the thoughts and desires and presence of God; to literally gnaw upon his Life as the Bread of Heaven. No longer are we to feed on our own flesh; instead we can receive the divine food of Christ that endures beyond this earth.

It is ours to choose what we eat.

---

[13] *John 6:64 (Amplified Bible)*

Don't just think of Him.
Feed on Him.
Eat His body.
Drink His blood,
until nothing of
your self is left
and He is all
in all of you.

THE TIE THAT BINDS

I heard once of a shocking custom in a primitive tribe. When someone in the group killed another, they strapped the dead body of the victim onto the back of the murderer until he eventually died, too. As I was thinking about forgiveness recently, this horrifying practice came to mind. It seemed to have a spiritual parallel.

The Bible says in 1 John 3:15, "Whosoever hates his brother is a murderer." And in 1 John 3:14, "He that loves not his brother abides in death." When we hold something in our heart against someone and will not forgive, we actually hate them. And the hatred binds us to them just as surely as love does.

Medical findings indicate that bitterness and unforgiveness can bring on all manner of disease. Could it be that those we hate and thus murder spiritually are bound to us, slowly poisoning our own body and soul, until we too are among the living dead?

This is a serious consideration, especially in light of the fact that in the Greek, the word "forgive" means to unbind.

Unfulfilled expectations make us bitter.
They break a sweet heart
and make it a quitter.
No longer will we freely give
to the offending friend.
No longer will we peacefully live
until forgiveness, our hearts can mend.

SAME OLD WAYS

There's no doubt about it. I'm disappointed I'm not a
saint. I grieve that I'm still vain, still a pleaser of people,
that I still too often do what pleases me instead of what
pleases God. I want to obey and seek his kingdom first,
but I don't always do it. I've got the same old ways I've
always had. I wonder why I don't change.

Could it be that God in his mercy keeps me from it?
Does he wait to change me until I want to change for
Him and not my self?

> Incorruptible seed,
> break through
> the husk of me.
> Break through
> my earth
> into the Light
> and bear fruit
> in my being.

SEPARATION

My friend recently separated from her husband. It was a long struggle over many years, but she finally made the decision. They were incompatible. He was insensitive to her needs, and she couldn't bear his faults. They didn't see many things the same way, and neither of them could tolerate the tension of their differences. It was a hopeless situation, one that had no apparent solution in togetherness.

St. Paul says in his first letter to the Corinthians that before one is married, one seeks to please the Lord, and after marriage—the husband or wife.[14] And so, he warns us, we who are married will have difficulty. In essence, then, it is as if we transfer our gaze from the Heavenly Beloved to the earthly spouse. He or she tends to supplant God as the center of our existence. We invest ourselves in our mate and then expect unconditional love and perfection in return, because these are the attributes of God.

My friend's husband is really a fine and decent man, no worse and no better than most of us. But he was in the position of God in her life, and when he disappointed her, all hell broke loose between them.

Both of them are relieved at the separation. He is out from under her criticism and she is free from the awful bondage of her dependence on him for her happiness.

---

[14] *1 Corinthians 7:32-35 (NKJV)*

Before, when she was looking to her husband for life, my friend was upset and insecure much of the time. Now she is no longer disappointed and angry when her husband doesn't live up to her expectations. She doesn't act like a fishwife when he does something boorish. She says she doesn't even judge him harshly in her heart anymore. Now she is able to have a "quiet spirit" and even appreciates her husband's humanness. He, in turn, no longer walks on eggs, resenting and fearing that he will displease his wife. In short, since my friend separated from her husband, both of them are happier for the arrangement.

What a pity, one might say, that these people had to separate to achieve harmony. And why can't they now get back together?

Actually, my friend never physically left her husband. When her marriage seemed impossibly difficult, she sought a relationship elsewhere. She turned to a former love and began to spend more and more time with him. As that relationship grew and fulfilled her needs, she was enabled to separate from her dependence and expectation of her husband.

Now she depends on another, One who can easily carry the weight of her expectations. *"My soul, wait thou only upon God; for my expectation is from Him,"*[15] she can say with the psalmist. Her divine spouse, unlike her very human husband, will never fail her. *"You will keep him in perfect peace, whose mind is stayed on You, because he*

---

[15] *Psalm 62:5 (KJV)*

trusts in You"[16] Since her separation, my friend is at peace.

"Separation" is an interesting word. In both the Hebrew and Greek it is the meaning of our word "holy". The saints' writings speak of detachment in much the same way. Both words imply that one is closer to God than to people or things or circumstances, and therefore not unduly perturbed by others' opinions, behavior or life's vicissitudes. One is separated, or set apart from these on account of a profound relationship with God.

When Joseph was sold into Egypt by his brothers, he must have had this separation, for instead of becoming bitter at the cruel deed done to him, he looked for God's plan in the matter. And Sarah, when Abraham passed her off as his sister, must have been "separated", for rather than becoming rebellious and angry, she obeyed her husband, *hoping in God*.

And so it is with my friend. Her hope and faith have returned where they belong. She is in the process of becoming closer to God than she is to man. She is yet the wife of her husband. They are one flesh, under the same roof. But in her spirit she is married to Christ. He is now the center of her life, and that has made all the difference.

---

[16] *Isaiah 26:3 (NKJV)*

When I look into your eyes
behind the shade of flesh,
behind the mask of lids
and see you there.
Oh, how my heart feels joy
that we should know each other—
you, you are so beautiful
behind that shade of flesh,
so clear, so true.
There is a joining closer
than that of body.
We are one in Him.
Is that it?
Is that you I see
so beautiful
behind the eye-lids...
Or is it Him?
Or should I say
is it him
or You...
looking through the eyes
of each of us...

FROG AND PRINCESS

It's easy to love someone when they're considerate of
your needs, kind, faithful and true. But what about
when they're inconsiderate, petty, self-centered, critical
and demanding? And what if the one it's easy to love
and the mean one are the same person? Isn't that what
usually happens when we marry? The one who seemed
like a perfect prince disappears and a frog takes his
place.

When a woman discovers her mate has a slimy side, it's a
shock and a huge disappointment. If a husband is seen
to have a roving eye, a foul mouth, a mean streak, or
some other repulsive trait, some women react with
railing and scorn, pointing out faults with self-righteous
gusto. Others, though they may be hurt and resentful
inside, ignore their husband's faults, even to the point of
covering them up. But neither of these responses help.
If we continually criticize our husbands, we become
harpies and they tune out our "helpful" insights, get
hostile, and marriage becomes war. If we are silent and
repress our criticism, keeping up a good front, our health
often suffers from stuffed rage.

What can we women do about the dilemma of being
married to imperfect men we don't seem able to change?
In the fairy tale, the princess kisses the frog and he
becomes a prince. This doesn't seem to happen in
ordinary life. Even if we are able to kiss the froggy
nature of our husband, our kisses are mere pecks that
have no transforming power. If there is a deep truth

spoken through the fairy tale, it doesn't seem to work for most of us. Why?

Could it be the frog is not the only one who needs transformation? It takes a real princess to kiss a frog and turn him into a prince. Am I a real princess? If I have given my life to God and He has adopted me into his royal line, I am a princess. But why do my attitude and actions more often reflect the gutter than the palace? And why do I find it so difficult to forgive my nearest neighbor/enemy, much less love him?

When we come to the end of our life on earth, it is not likely that we will have to give an account of our husband's faults. It is more likely that in the light of God we will see our own failure to manifest his unconditional love. Our human love is subject to mood and circumstance and when we are scorned, turns into hate. Only God's love endures.

A real princess lives in the palace and spends time with the King. She knows Him intimately, learns his ways, and is filled with his spirit. Because her deepest needs are fulfilled by the love of the Perfect One, she no longer expects perfection from her mate. When she sees his flaws, she cries out to the King to help him. In this way she becomes an intercessor for her husband and not an accuser. And the King answers her prayers by giving her the gift of his compassion. Then she becomes a real princess. And then she is able to kiss her frog with the transforming power of Real Love, and free him to become the prince he was created to be.

GINGER PRESERVES AND AFGHAN BREAD

In the early days of our marriage I discovered my husband was somewhat of a hoarder. He was always afraid of running out of things and liked to keep a plentiful supply of everything. I, in turn, as a fairly new Christian had become so "spiritual" that I was, as the saying goes, "no earthly good". We were an interesting couple. He worried that I wouldn't have stocked up on his favorite foods, and I worried that the spiritual communication we had enjoyed before marriage had been reduced to butter, eggs and ginger preserves.

My husband loved ginger preserves, especially on toasted Afghan bread. One morning he asked me to buy more Afghan bread that day as we were out of it. Since "out" for him usually meant we only had one of something left, I ignored his request. But that evening when he asked for his desert of Afghan bread and ginger preserves, I discovered he had been right—we were out of Afghan bread. Fortunately, I found a lone stale piece in the refrigerator, toasted it and presented it to my husband. He happily slathered it with ginger preserves and commented that we were almost running out of ginger preserves and he wished I would buy more.

At that point inwardly I started to complain to myself "There he goes again..." when by some special grace my thoughts took a different direction. Suddenly a play I had once read came to mind. The plot was about a woman who fell in love with a man's angel. But when she married and was confronted with her husband's fleshy nature was very unhappy. She only loved her husband when his angel was present. Somehow the conflict was resolved when the angel visited her with the message that her task on earth was to accept and love the very ordinary part of her husband. I couldn't stand this play because it wasn't "spiritual" enough for me. I think I also disliked it because it described who I was and I was not willing then to acknowledge this.

I have always known and loved a noble spirit in my husband—one with clear, wise eyes, kind, humorous, and uncompromising in his sense of truth. Anything less than this I have not believed was my husband, and often with axe and chisel in hand have chipped away at the unreal, earthy, less than perfect crustation. To accept and love the "unspiritual" jelly-loving, petty-anxiety-ridden creature has been an aim foreign to the high and mighty me. And I have done a lot of lecturing in my day while grudgingly catering to my husband's "whims" (the things he thinks are important and I don't). In fact it has seemed my duty to show my husband the unimportance of ordinary things he thinks important, and to convince him of the "Really Important Things". But if love has to do with accepting a person as they are and not trying to change them, and when they ask for bread not giving them a stone (not even the rock of truth) ... if love has to do with these things, I have done little loving.

God doesn't require us to come up higher before he accepts us. The message of the Cross is that God comes to us where we are. This is what gives us hope and freedom to change. Why can't we be this way with each other? *"You will know the truth and the truth shall set you free,"*[17] scripture says. The truth is that in Christ we are accepted in the Beloved no matter our ordinary and worse than ordinary condition. I knew this once when I first came to Him in my need and He met me. I knew then that I and everyone else was ordinary but that He met us in the ordinary, hallowing it, making it extra-ordinary. What made me forget this? Ah yes—I got "spiritual".

No wonder I didn't like that play. I didn't want to come down from the heights where I lived as a puffed-up new convert. I didn't want to accept myself and others as we are and humbly give back on earth the love received from heaven. And I didn't understand that love is expressed in ordinary things—like ginger preserves and Afghan bread.

---

[17] *John 8:32 (NIV)*

I expect of you.
You expect of me.
When each of us gives,
there is harmony.
But if I give to you
and you don't give back,
there may be hell to pay
for the love I lack.

ALL THINGS FLEE THEE...

This Christmas I received a rich gift—I was neglected by both friends and family. On Christmas day, which is also our anniversary, my husband neither gave me a token of remembrance nor acknowledged that we had been married that day over twenty years ago. Relatives in whom I have invested myself neither called nor sent cards. Friends I gave thoughtful gifts to did not give in return or even respond adequately to my "thoughtfulness." Inwardly I felt bereft—uncared for and unappreciated.

It was only after going through considerable throes of self-pity that the line from Francis Thompson's poem, *The Hound of Heaven* came to me. "All things flee thee that fleest me." On the holiday we call Christmas I was feeling forsaken by man—and I had forsaken the One whom Christmas is all about. It was his birthday or at least the day we celebrate his coming to earth. And I, part of his family, in whom He had invested Himself—in fact, for whom He had laid down his life—had forgotten Him.

All those cookies and cards and fussy festive doings of Christmas I had been caught up in had left me no time or attention for the Lord. There was no room in my inner life; it was too filled with little do-goodings. In short I had neglected my First Love and He had graciously allowed me to realize it by holding back the care of friends and family. Of course He is not so petty to be jealous as we are jealous. In his compassion when his own have strayed from the path that leads to Life, we are allowed to discover our misdirection by feeling a few thorns in the briar patch of human expectation.

I have a friend who does not see his dealings in this way. She often accuses me of anthropomorphizing God, and I am prone to listen to her sensible-sounding voice and think perhaps I imagine the imprint of his hand in circumstances. But in this instance I found it interesting to note that after the holidays were over and I had remembered my first Love, my husband remembered me; phone calls from friends, and cards and tokens which had been delayed or mysteriously gone astray were delivered. But by then these expressions of people's care didn't matter so much, for I had returned to the Beloved and knew his caring.

His gifts to us come not always in pretty packages. Expectation of man inevitably brings painful disappointments. But when these turn us to God who is the source of our being's true hope, they are gifts of inestimable value.

Help Lord,
its happening again—
I'm more real to me
then You are.

THREE VIEWS OF MARRIAGE

COMPLAINT OF A NEW WIFE

Lord, he's not what I thought.
He's bumptious, self-centered, a bit of an ass.
And when no one is looking,
his actions are crass.
Before our marriage he was a shining knight.
Now, I confess, I can't stand his sight.
And now it's so apparent
that anyone can see
he loves himself more
than he ever loved me!

LAMENT OF A NEW HUSBAND

O Lord, I long to be treated
with some respect,
but my wife doesn't give it
as I was led to expect.
She exposes all my faults
and rolls her eyes at me,
often behind my back
so everyone can see.

Lord, it's hard to be married
to such a wife
and I dread to think
of the rest of my life.

COUNSEL FROM AN
OLD MARRIED COUPLE

Learn from us, you two.
We are of the same flesh,
we have been like you.
We have seen in each other
all the faults and lack.
We have criticized, complained
and done the same back.
We wasted many years
in this darkened state,
feeling pity for ourselves
and moaning our fate.
Then into our dark Light came.
We found the Word of God
and our lives were not the same.

We saw marriage as a mirror
in which we get to see
the frailties and faults
of the person we call "me".
We stopped looking at our mate
through eyes of the accuser.
We stopped listening to his hate.
We stopped being his abuser.
We started confessing our own faults
and praying for our spouse.
And now the peace of God
reigns throughout our house.

PRAISE FROM THE PIT

Naked praise is best.
Unadorned by sight or feeling
it rises pure and straight
to the Father.
It adores the Father for Himself –
not what he has done
or will do...
For down in the pit's black
with the low earth spirits
pulling and distracting
one cannot remember
what He has done
and there is no hope even
of what He will do.
One can only cling
to his Presence
and give up.

This is what our Lord did
when He was crucified...
In the midst of unspeakable suffering
He gave up his spirit to the Father.
That is our work, too.
and it is true praise.

"LOVE ONE ANOTHER AS I HAVE LOVED YOU"*

The infinite wisdom of Christ—to give us a command impossible for the outer man to fulfill: He literally went to the heart of the matter. For it is in our hearts where true religion lives. If I am one who is able to obey the Ten Commandments outwardly, I may avoid facing the fact of my sin. But to be given a command to *"Love one another as I have loved you"*—this brings me to my knees, crying out to God.[18] For that kind of love is not humanly possible. When we are loved and appreciated, it is easy to respond with love. But let us be scorned, ill-treated, or even just unappreciated, and what we thought was love turns to something quite other. How blessed we are to have this commandment of Jesus, for it brings us to reality. We cannot love if we reside in our ordinary flesh nature. Only Christ in us can truly love. All the other is masquerade or delusion, and when the situation is extreme enough, we hate the very ones we thought we loved.

When we have eyes to see that this is our condition, in humility we will move inward to that secret place of the Most High where True Love resides.

---

[18] *John 13:34 (NIV)*

Go in, go in
There lies no sin
'Tis holy ground.
Hush, make no sound.
Only go in.
Whatever the price, pay it.
Whatever the price, pay it.
Only go in.

BODY OF CHRIST

Merle Maupin was over 70 years old when he first visited our fellowship in Virginia. He had recently been baptized in the Holy Spirit and appeared in our body of believers glowing with the light of God. He had been a Baptist minister most of his life and was then retired. In his youth he had performed on the piano for silent films and he had a gift for playing with great sensitivity and gusto. He would worship and play with his open bible on the top of the piano and when he finished a discernible presence of the Holy Spirit held the room in silence until the gathering broke into vocal worship. He manifested a great joy which drew some of us to him like moths to a flame of fire. I didn't know him well but I recognized his authentic humanity and delighted when he made the trip from his home in North Carolina to Virginia.

Not too long after we met him, my husband and I moved from the country and then were not connected to any church. One Sunday I was experiencing severe allergies and depression. I recall wishing for someone who would understand what I was going through and asking the Lord lightly, not with intensity or much faith, for someone like this who could phone me. Later on that day, Merle Maupin called me from North Carolina. He said that he has been trying all day to get our number because the Lord had put me on his heart so strongly that he knew he was to call. My faith level was so low then that I was shocked. The little prayer of my heart had been answered—God had heard my cry. I don't remember my conversation with Merle then—it was the connection with God, the Head, who had heard the need of one of his body and communicated it to another that meant most to me and raised my faith.

When later we moved back to the country, I learned one of the secrets of his joy and hearing ear; he got up at 3:30 each morning to be with the Lord to worship and listen and pray. When I think of the Body of Christ there are many wonderful caring friends who come to mind, but Merle Maupin especially exemplifies the invisible Body on earth that has ears to hear from the Head in Heaven.

Friends in Christ
are not constrained
by time or space.
For the spirit
knows no bounds
of years or place.
Those who know Him
belong to each other,
for He is their head
and He is their brother.
They are His body
born from Above;
of the same Father,
formed by His love.
So wherever you are,
nothing can sever
our bonds in Him
who is with us forever.

THE LIE AND THE TRUTH

If we believe the lie that God is a merciless judge with a hatchet in his hand and a scowl on his face, we will live in constant tension seeking to please this hard taskmaster and never succeeding. Fear will be our dominant emotion and we will be tormented creatures because *"fear has torment."*[19]

And if we who have experienced the unspeakable mercy of Christ can be made to forget that mercy and become stern moralists according to this false image, then the devil wins twice: he blurs our own vision of the Truth and by our negative legalism gets us to manifest the bad news that God is unrelenting hard, while we mouth the "good news" with our lips.

And who will be attracted to this gospel? If I must be perfect to be accepted, life is a continual walking on eggshells, and the time of my days spent in wiping egg off my feet. That is not good news. And after a while those who believe this lie will give up walking at all and settle down in a dark corner and give up.

If we who have been saved by his mercy would believe and manifest the Truth that God is Love and Christ is with us, the forces of Satan would lose their power in our lives. For then out of heart response to this vast but immanent One who loves us, we would worship.

---

[19] *1 John 4:18 (KJV)*

This is what the enemy fears most. For true worship opens us to hearing God and being led by his Spirit.

In the morning,
in the night,
in the darkness
and the light.
In life's sorrow
and life's joy –
praise Him.

LETTING GO

Before one can know the reality of the realm of God there seems to be a necessity for some sort of surrender of the self. We give up to God because we need his action and see the inadequacy of our own. Then we experience his grace and new life. But after a while the old life surfaces again and we shift back into our own gear trying to "do" of our selves. Jesus said, *"Without Me you can do nothing."*[20] Why then do some of us continue to try to "do"—even good works—on our own?

I wonder sometimes if this is an inevitable phase that must be passed through before we are ready for the Master's table. When fish are caught, they thrash back and forth before they die and can be eaten. When we are caught by the hook of God, are we too in this process? And does He patiently wait until all our thrashing has ceased and we are dead to our self-activity?

And is it only then when we have really let go that He can feed us to the multitude of hungering ones?

---

[20] *John 15:5 (KJV)*

O my God,
free me from my bonds
when You see
I am ready
to follow You...
when I will not
deviate from your path
into the wilds
of the world,
the evil one,
or my self.

Every step that I take – let it be Yours.
Every move that I make – let it be Yours.
Every prayer that I pray – let it be Yours.
Every word that I say – let it be Yours.

Oh Father – me too.
Let me be Yours.

www.ingramcontent.com/pod-product-compliance
Lightning Source LLC
Chambersburg PA
CBHW060533030426
42337CB00021B/4234